BOWLING GREEN STATE UNIVERSITY
DISCARDED
LIBRARY
CURRICULUM RESOURCE CENTER
BOWLING GREEN STATE UNIVERSITY
BOWLING GREEN, OHIO 43403

TRACTORS

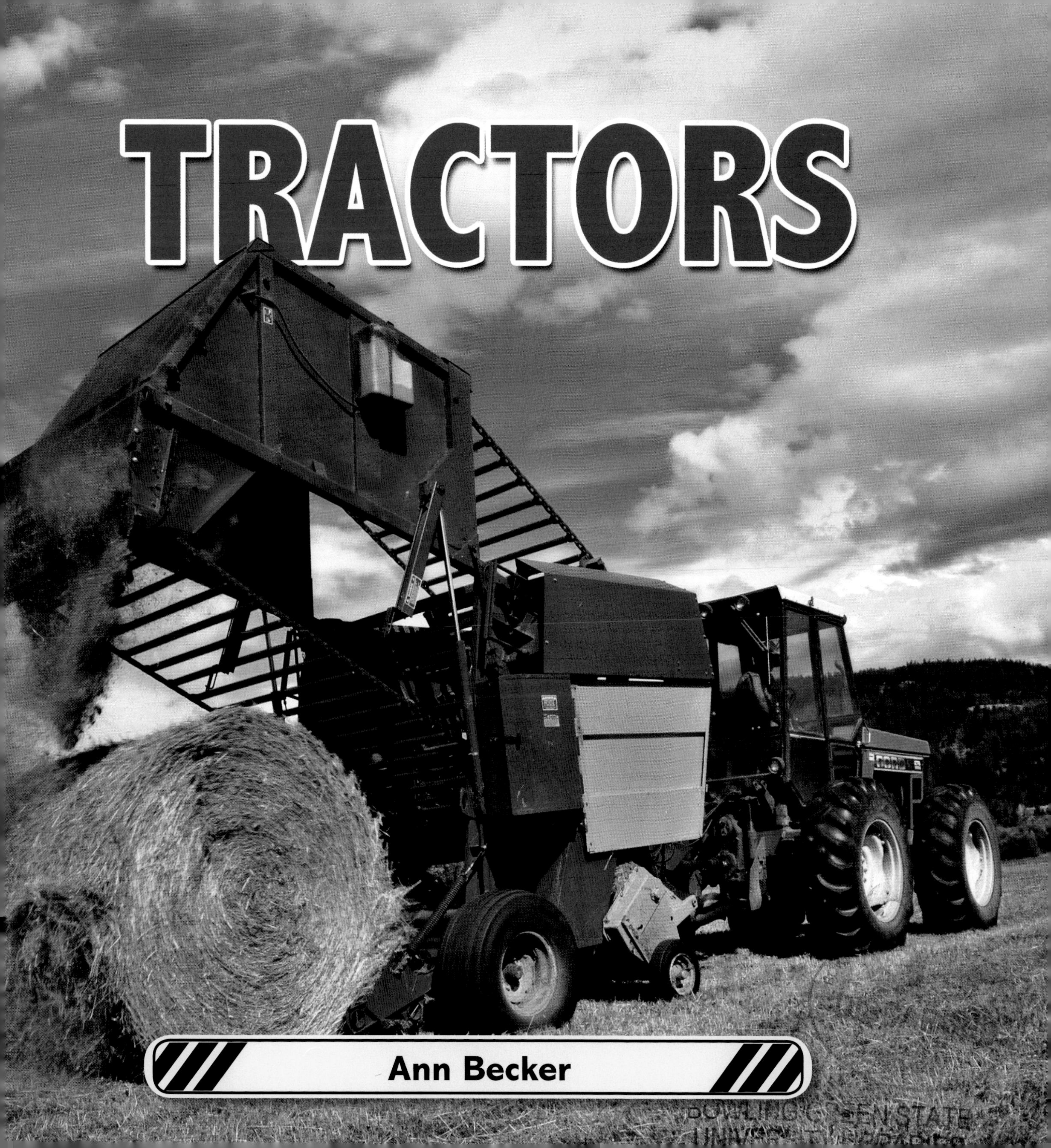

Ann Becker

This edition first published in 2010 in the United States of America by Marshall Cavendish Benchmark.

Marshall Cavendish Benchmark
99 White Plains Road
Tarrytown, NY 10591
www.marshallcavendish.us

All Internet addresses were available and accurate when this book was sent to press.

Library of Congress Cataloging-in-Publication Data

Becker, Ann, 1965-
Tractors / by Ann Becker.
p. cm. -- (Amazing machines)
Summary: "Discusses the different kinds of tractors, what they are used for, and how they work"--Provided by publisher.
Includes bibliographical references and index.
ISBN 978-0-7614-4406-0
1. Tractors--Juvenile literature. I. Title.
TL233.15.B43 2010
629.225'2--dc22
2008054371

The photographs in this book are used by permission and through the courtesy of:
t=top b=bottom c=center l=left r=right m=middle
Cover Photos: Santosha/ iStockphoto; (Inset): iStockphoto
Title Photo: Cameronpashak/iStockphoto
Content Page: Maga/Shutterstock

4-5: Olly/Shutterstock; 6-7: Danilo Calilung/Corbis; 7(inset): Comstock Select/Corbis; 8-9: Kenway/Dreamstime; 9(inset): Craig Lovell /Eagle Visions Photography; 10(inset): Rhoberazzi/iStockphoto; 10-11: Lorraine Swanson/123rf; 12-13: Tony Hertz/Alamy; 13(inset): mrfotos/iStockphoto; 14-15: Foodanddrinkphotos/Photolibrary; 15(inset): Mike McEnnerney/Alamy; 16-17BG: Maga/Shutterstock; 16(inset): Christophe Boisvieux/Corbis; 16-17: Marcel Jancovic/Shutterstock; 18(inset): Cameronpashak/iStockphoto; 18-19: Eric Boegel/iStockphoto; 20-21: Eric Boegel/Shutterstock; 21(inset): Vandervelden/iStockphoto; 22-23: Robert Read/Alamy; 23(inset): J.schultes/Dreamstime; 24-25: Danusia/Dreamstime; 25(inset): NASA ; 26-27BG: Javarman /Shutterstock; 26L: J.schultes/Dreamstime; 26R: Mike McEnnerney /Alamy; 27T: Lorraine Swanson/123rf; 27B: Cameronpashak/iStockphoto; 28-29BG: maga/Shutterstock; 28-29: Eric Boegel/iStockphoto; 30-31BG: Maga/Shutterstock; 30-31: Marcel Jancovic/Shutterstock; 32BG: Maga/Shutterstock

Art Director: Sumit Charles

Client Service Manager: Santosh Vasudevan

Project Manager: Shekhar Kapur

Editor: Penny Dowdy

Designer: Ritu Chopra

Photo Researcher: Shreya Sharma

Printed in Malaysia

1 3 5 6 4 2

Contents

What Is a Tractor?

A tractor is a machine that pulls or pushes a tool over land. When you think of a tractor, you usually think of farm equipment.

Farmers rely a lot on tractors. They use them to plant and **harvest** crops. But tractors have many other uses, too.

This tractor pulls a trailer on a large farm.

Utility Tractor

Utility tractors are used all around your neighborhood. They pull lawn mower blades, rakes, or wagons. They are so popular that most local hardware stores sell them.

Tractors can pick up golf balls lost on a golf course.

People who have large yards use utility tractors to mow their lawns and pick up the cut grass. Utility tractors are used at school, too. They can mow ball fields and even carry a team's sports equipment.

These containers catch the grass that the tractor cuts.

This utility tractor mows a family lawn.

Row Crop Tractor

A **row crop tractor** is more powerful than a utility tractor. It is especially designed for farms. It sits tall to pass over rows of crops.

This is the cab where the driver sits.

The wheels on the row crop tractor are very tall!

The hitch holds the tools that the tractor pulls.

Row crop tractors can pull a variety of tools. Some tools might clean out weeds between rows. Others might cut down crops at the end of the season.

This row crop tractor has a tool for planting seeds.

This tractor is pulling blades that mow down plants.

Combine

A **combine** is a tractor that combines two jobs. It cuts down plants and also removes the grain from the stems. A row crop tractor would need two tools to do these jobs.

The thresher removes the grain from the plant.

The chopper cuts the plant off the ground.

Before tractors had engines, horses pulled machines like this harvester.

Combines have different settings for different plants. Grains of wheat are small, and ears of corn are large. A farmer can use a combine to harvest both kinds of plants.

Combines can save farmers time by doing two jobs at once.

Sprayer Tractor

Sprayer tractors spray water, bug spray, or plant food on crops. Sprayers can be the only job of a tractor, or a sprayer can be added to a row crop tractor.

The boom holds all of the hoses.

Each hose sprays on the plants.

Sprayers come in many sizes. Some are very wide so that farmers can spray many rows of crops at one time. Smaller sprayers are used for smaller fields.

This sprayer is built for spraying narrow rows.

This tractor is only made to spray.

This sprayer covers many rows at one time.

Planter Tractor

Planter tractors do just what the name describes — they plant. Planter tractors plant seed or seedlings.

The seed is stored in this big bucket.

Farmers can change how close the planter drops the seeds or seedlings. Planters can make wide rows, narrow rows, or something in between. This helps farmers plant each crop just right.

The machine shoots seeds out of the planter.

The tiller scratches rows into the soil.

Birds stay near this planter to eat some of the seeds.

This planter tractor plants seeds, not seedlings.

Tiller Tractor

Tiller tractors loosen the soil to make it ready for planting. It's important that soil be loose so that seeds can grow. Water can seep into loose soil better than hard soil.

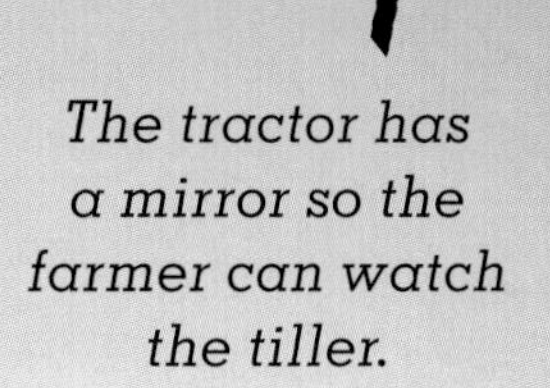

The tractor has a mirror so the farmer can watch the tiller.

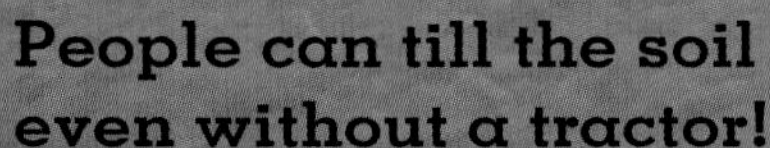

People can till the soil even without a tractor!

Some tiller tractors have seeders attached to them to save time. This means the tractor first breaks up the hard soil, then drops the seed into the ground.

This tiller has a seeder to save time.

The chisel breaks up the soil.

This tiller tractor does not dig very deep. The seeds must be very small!

Loader Tractor

Loader tractors can pick up and move loads. Loads are simply anything that a truck, wagon, or tractor might carry.

This tractor has a tool that makes bales, or loads, of hay.

Farmers often use loader tractors to carry bales of hay. They may move the hay from the field where it is grown to trucks that take it to market. Or they may take the hay to their **pastures** for their animals to eat.

The spears on this loader can poke right into a bale of hay.

The boom of the loader is strong enough to lift heavy loads in the air.

This loader tractor could pull another tool in the back.

Cutter Tractor

A **cutter tractor** cuts and shreds grass and weeds. The cutter may be a tractor on its own, or it may be pulled behind a row crop tractor.

Tractors need powerful engines to do such hard work.

These steps help the farmer climb into the cab.

Cutter tractors are like giant lawn mowers. Farmers use them to mow their pastures. They also use them to clear new fields where they want to plant crops.

This cutter has a shredder.

This row crop tractor pulls the cutter.

Tedder

Tedder is a name for a big rake. Animals will not eat wet hay. A tedder tractor fluffs the hay so it will dry out.

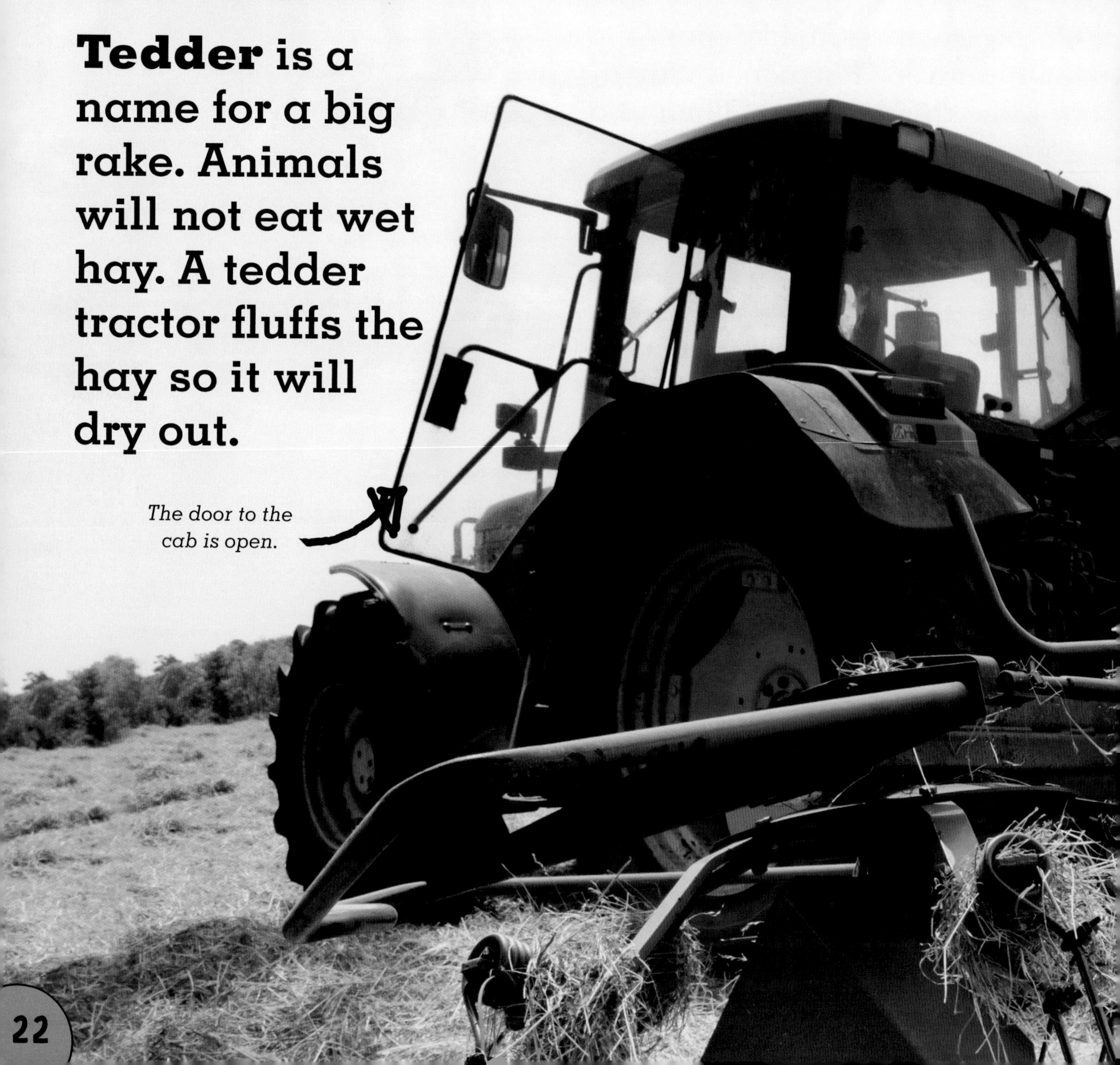

The door to the cab is open.

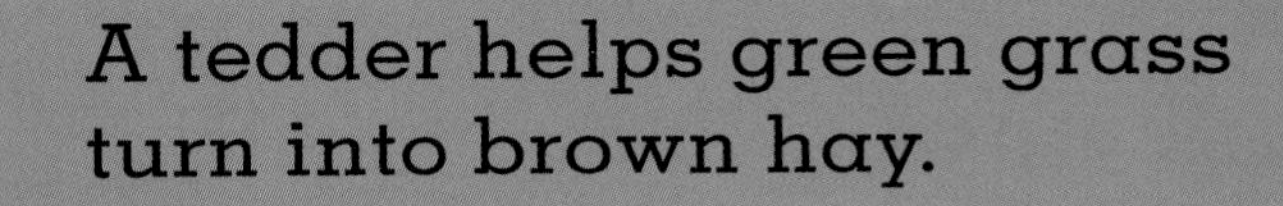
A tedder helps green grass turn into brown hay.

Some tedders look like huge rakes on wheels. They pull straight through the field. Other tedders look like spiders. They spin in circles as the tractor drives through the fields

Hay is grass that is dried out.

This old tedder spun the hay to fluff it.

These prongs work like a big rake.

Tractor Crawler

A **tractor crawler** does not have wheels. It has caterpillar tracks. They hold the ground tightly.

This tractor crawler can carry many people on its back.

The driver sits in the cab.

These caterpillar tracks can hold tight on slippery ice and snow.

The same idea that makes the tractor crawler work is used to move huge rockets and the Space Shuttle.

Look below the Space Shuttle. That is a huge tractor crawler.

Many machines use caterpillar tracks to hold the ground.

Summing Up

Tractors help farmers do their jobs every day. Tractors dig, plant, mow, and harvest crops. They also help people with large yards and gardens.

Tractors are not only helpful with crops. They can plow snow and carry giant machines like the Space Shuttle!

Combine

Loader

Amazing Facts

- Some tractors have smaller front wheels than back wheels. This allows the tractor to turn in small circles.
- Tractors can be dangerous! One-third of accidents on farms happen with tractors and other farm machines.
- John Deere built his first plow shop in 1848. Deere & Company has 52,000 employees today.
- The country with the most tractors per acre is Iceland.

- The National Farm Machinery Show displays the newest tractors and farm tools each year.

- At a tractor pull, drivers compete to see whose tractor can pull a heavy load the farthest.

Glossary

combine a tractor that cuts down a plant and also removes the grain

cutter tractor a tractor that cuts down and shreds grass or weeds

harvest to pick or cut down a crop

loader tractor a tractor that carries and moves loads such as hay

pasture a field of grass for farm animals

planter tractor a tractor that plants seeds or seedlings

row crop tractor a tractor that is tall enough to drive over crops

sprayer tractor a tractor that sprays crops with water, bug spray, or plant food

tedder a tractor that rakes or fluffs hay

tiller tractor a tractor that breaks up or loosens soil

tractor crawler a tractor that has caterpillar tracks instead of wheels

utility tractor a small tractor that pulls tools

Index

Web Finder

http://www.deere.com/en_US/compinfo/kidscorner/home.html

http://www.cbc.ca/kidscbc/play.php#tractorTomPaint

http://www.yesterdaystractors.com/kids.htm

http://www.valdosta.edu/~hhall/topic.html